COSMIEL'S GIFT

an excerpt from *The Prophecies*

PHILIP CARR-GOMM

with images by
ANGELA LEMAIRE

Published by The Oak Tree Press 2016

PO Box 1333, Lewes, East Sussex, BN7 1DX
England

Tel/Fax +44 (0)1273 470888 Email
office@druidry.org

All rights reserved. The right of Philip Carr-Gomm to be identified as the author of this work has been asserted by him in accordance with the Copyright, Designs and Patents Act, 1988.

Copyright © 2016 Philip Carr-Gomm

Images © 2016 Angela Lemaire

ISBN: 1903232058

ISBN-13: 978-1-903232-05-7

PREFACE

Cosmiel's Gift is a small part of a story that began to take shape ten years ago when I first visited the mysterious forest of Brocéliande in Brittany. I found the grail church created by Abbé Henri Gillard at the edge of the forest, and soon discovered that a woman, known as the Druidess of Brocéliande, had lived nearby during the Second World War.

I was told that she had a lover, a German Luftwaffe pilot, but although there was an airforce base nearby, I was unable to confirm whether or not this was true.

I decided to write a story, *The Prophecies*, based on the lives of the Druidess, Geneviève Zaepffel, and the priest Henri Gillard, with the addition of a fictional character - Hermann Kaestner, an idealistic young German officer. The resulting book deals with the themes of delusion and obsession, love, betrayal and redemption, set against the background of occupied France, with its strange climate of part-collaboration, part-resistance, and an unfortunately widespread sentiment of anti-semitism.

In the story, 'Cosmiel's Gift' forms an entry in Hermann's notebook, which his sister reads after the war. If you haven't yet read *The Prophecies*, you may want to wait until you have read the book before you turn the following pages.

The account of the *post-mortem* journey that is described here is inspired by early Jewish Merkabah mysticism, and by the book 'The Ecstatic Journey' by the 17th century Jesuit polymath Athanasius Kircher, who describes a journey through the cosmos accompanied by the angel Cosmiel.

Frontispiece to Kircher's 1671 *Iter Exstaticum* depicting Kircher accompanied by the angel Cosmiel on a journey through the cosmos.

According to the website amunaor.com: "The word Merkaba can be broken down thus: MER: rotating fields of light, KA: spirit, and BA: soul (this is taken from an 18th dynasty Egyptian translation, and in Hebrew it means 'Chariot'). Therefore, Mer-Ka-Ba means the spirit or energy body surrounded by counter-rotating fields of light, or spirals of energy (as with a strand of DNA), which transport spirit or consciousness from one dimension to another.

"It became an object of visionary contemplation for Jewish mystics in Palestine in the 1st century AD; in the 7th–11th century, Merkabah mysticism was centered in Babylonia.

"Merkabah mystics courted ecstatic visions that involved a dangerous ascent through celestial hierarchies to the throne of God. Hostile angels guarded the gates to the seven "heavenly dwellings," and a successful journey required magical formulas."

COSMIEL'S GIFT

*How can I find the Mystery in the light where everything can be seen? Only the unknown can give birth, and the unknown lives in the darkness,
and the silence.*

*Give me more,
you might say.
But I can only give it to you
out of the darkness of my being.*

I dreamt the other night that I died. My plane crashed as I was flying over the Manoir. There was a jolt, the shock of the plane hitting the ground, and all at once I was with Geneviève at the window and I could feel her body close to mine, and I looked out across the fields and saw the plane coming out of a clear sky.

I thought, "It hasn't crashed. How strange." I was so happy to be with her, and we could have been standing there for eternity - our hearts wide open to the heavens.

Then I saw the plane plunging to earth and I heard the explosion and saw the flames, and I even saw myself sitting in the cockpit. I felt no shock myself, but I felt it hit Geneviève like a wave. And I reached out towards her to hold her close, but found I couldn't feel her body any more - she was no longer solid. My arm just slipped through her as if she wasn't really there. She started sobbing and I wanted to console her and say 'It's alright, I'm here. It's alright, I'm alive! Can't you see me?' But I knew what was happening. I was dying or perhaps I was already dead. I found myself being pulled upwards. I reached out, but

Geneviève, the Manoir, the wreckage of the plane, all dropped away from me. All that I could see, all that was on Earth, became toys, miniature copies of real things that kept getting smaller and smaller, until I could no longer see them.

And then I could see nothing. I was sinking into my mother's arms as a child, a warm bath, the embrace of night. Soon there were dreams - dreams within my dream. Sometimes beautiful, sometimes dark and terrifying

In the dark times I would feel as if I was drugged - paralyzed, unable to move, unable to run away. I saw all the hatred and horror of war paraded before me - wounded soldiers crying out in pain, faces of countless men, women, children, being killed in the prison camps. I would shake with sorrow, my heart unable to bear the enormity of the suffering until I sensed a presence beside me. At first I thought it was my mother or father and they would reassure me, but then the presence would seem to be neither of them, but something more, something that could take on different masks whenever it wished, and it would soothe me with singing. And then it was that I discovered the identity of this being who could wear so many masks: it was my Guardian Angel, whose name, he told me, was Cosmiel.

He said it was foolish to think of him as male or female, and that I shouldn't even bother too much about his or her name, because what was more important was the gift he was about to give me.

"In my world we can become anything we wish," he said, "and I am wishing now that I am a river." And he smiled at me with such love, and stretched out and held my head in his hands, and I began to feel as if I was floating on the river he had become, and it was broad and wide, and the water that flowed along this river was made of love. And as I floated along, I heard Cosmiel speaking to me: "This is the river of the Holy Grail, the well-spring of life. This is the Ganges, the Brahmaputra, the river Boyne, the Jordan, the sacred Nile."

I looked at the river bank, and I could see children playing in the reeds. They were laughing as they splashed about in the water. Some of them had found a basket, and an older boy carried it up on to the bank. I drifted over and climbed out, and together with the children, we watched as the boy took out a knife and carefully cut through the black leather cover that sealed the basket. And then all at once I was lying in that basket, and his knife had cut away all the sadness, all the pain of my past, and I was a naked baby lying fresh and new, the sunlight playing on my eyes. And then I woke up.

Cosmiel felt so real to me, I tried at once to communicate with him. I lay in bed and imagined he was sitting beside me. I confessed to him all that I had wanted to confess to Father Gillard, but couldn't, and once I had told him everything, every foolish mistake, every betrayal and stupidity I had committed, I could feel that something was being freed inside me. It was as if a weight, or rather many weights attached to tangled cords that had wrapped themselves around me, were slipping away.

Cosmiel must have known this was happening because he said, "It's like that here, you know, in the world beyond death. Things just fall away from you - you can't tell when. The nightmares stop, being gripped by fear and regret stops, and you find it's all been stripped back, stripped away, through love and forgetting and forgiving, and reliving over and over, and that's when you can begin your voyage through the sea of stars."

I started to fall asleep again, but my memory of what happened whilst I slept was crystal clear when I awoke.

Cosmiel said to me, "Let me show you the journey you will take when you leave this world. This will make it easier for you when your time comes. I do this in the spirit of the Austrian monk Abraham a Sancta Clara who wrote: 'If you die before you die, then when you die, you will not die.' "

To do this, Cosmiel said we should go to St Onenne's well. And all at once I was in Tréhorenteuc, following my Guardian Angel as he moved silently down that familiar road, past Harel's, along that lane between the rectory and the Mairie.

When we got to the well, its surface was covered in hawthorn blossom. "Best to go quickly," said Cosmiel, who dived into the pool and disappeared beneath the flowers. After only a second of hesitation I followed.

We were both travelling through what at first I thought was water. It was dark, and to move forward I had to swim. I was a fish, a baby born in the sea, a dolphin on the wave, and just ahead of me swam Cosmiel.

As I followed him, I started to see gleaming lights, phosphorescent fish perhaps, underwater fireflies, but as we swam further I realized this was not water we were swimming through, but Space Herself in all her dark majesty.

After some time, as we slowly traversed the ocean of Space, the moon came into view - a vast white sphere glowing with such brightness I could hardly look ahead. No longer were we swimming in darkness, we were swimming in light, in the milk of Isis. And gradually the Moon grew larger and larger until I realized we were going to land on its surface.

As we came closer, I saw that we were coming to rest beside two silver pomegranate trees in the gardens of a great palace, carved in white marble and moonstone. Cosmiel beckoned me to follow him up a flight of stairs that led towards the entrance. Beside its doors stood a tall naked man, who said at once, "Do not be surprised. This is the place of divestment - the first sphere of cleansing."

And I looked at my body and I saw that I still had clothing on - trousers, shoes, a shirt. He said, "Leave all of these here by the door. As you remove each one you will feel yourself becoming lighter, freer. Then walk forward. Walk into the palace-temple."

And it was there that I underwent my first initiation. I was challenged by an angel swathed in grey mist whose eyes glowed with a preternatural light. He told me to cover myself for shame, and urged me to dress again, to keep my clothes, because they were now all I possessed in the world. I laughed at him, and he finally laughed too and allowed me into the inner sanctum. There another angel stood, with a calm and radiant countenance, and she told me that the sphere of the moon is the realm of the etheric, the energy field that enlivens our physical being. With gestures of her hand around my body, which left me mesmerised with their grace, she took all that I had learnt and experienced in my energy body, and poured the resulting distillation into a silver cup, which she then offered to my lips.

As I drank the liquid, my etheric body fell from me as the last clothing falls from the beloved when she enters the bed chamber.

Cosmiel took me by the hand and led me from the temple, until we were standing beside the pomegranate trees in the garden. "Walk between the trees slowly with me," he said, and as we did this, it was as if our feet had wings and we were lifted up into the air, and we journeyed higher and higher through space as we made our way to the Second Heaven, which was on the planet Mercury.

Already I was changed. Without my etheric body, I flew with Cosmiel as fast as thought itself. And when he and I came to stand at the entrance to the temple-palace of Mercury, we were met by a man with the head of a bird, who ushered us into the outer chamber, where I was challenged at the point of a sword by the dark angel of Mercury. "Hold fast to your mind, old friend," said the angel, "or you might lose it." And for a moment the fear of losing all my memories, all my cherished thoughts and visions, terrified me, until I saw a light in his eye, and I could laugh with scorn at his attempt to frighten me. He laughed too, and lowering his sword beckoned me forward.

And it was here, in my second initiation, that I was stripped of my thinking-self. All that I had thought, all those opinions I had formed, those theories about life and about how the world worked, I cast aside as easily as one would cast aside a pair of old spectacles no longer needed. All that I had learned, all that I had ever conceived, was distilled and handed to me as an elixir in a phial of crystal by an angel standing before me. I drank the elixir, and Cosmiel took me by the hand and we journeyed through space to the Third Heaven, which was on the planet Venus.

Freed of two sheaths that had covered my inner being, our travel to this planet was but a moment. As Cosmiel and I landed before the gates of the temple of Venus, we were met by a tall naked woman who handed me a single rose. She showed me into a circular room with a domed roof and invited me to lie on a couch that stood in the centre. As I lay there, she placed her palm on my forehead, and it was as if every dream, everything I had ever imagined or desired, was shown to me in succession in glorious and radiant colour. She lifted her palm from my forehead, I opened my eyes, and I watched as, with just a movement of her hand, all these images were reduced to but one translucent drop of perfume, which she touched to my brow.

After resting for moments which seemed to last an eternity, Cosmiel took me by the hand and we journeyed through space to the Fourth Heaven, which was on the Sun itself.

We walked towards its temple with joy in our hearts. A child was waiting for us, seated naked on a white horse, pointing to the entrance to the temple, made from sheets of burnished gold. But I will write no more of what happened there, for each of us is challenged in the depths of our heart in a different way, known only to our soul and our Guardian Angel. And in like manner, each of us receives in our own way the ecstasies of love and the illumination of this sphere.

From the Sun we travelled, Cosmiel and I, to Mars and Jupiter and Saturn, and in each sphere I was challenged and I was freed. I was reduced, and in reduction I was enlarged in love and in clarity of perception, until we travelled beyond the Seventh Heaven and entered the worlds of the zodiac and the *Primum Mobile*, the Place of Beginnings.

And it was in this place beyond Time, beyond even the confines of Space, that I came to know that at some stage after my death I would make the return journey, taking on the tasks and virtues of the angels of each sphere, gradually clothing my soul with the materials needed to think and feel on Earth again, so that when my mother gives birth to me, I will have a physical body drawn from the elements of this planet, an energy body of the Moon, a thinking self guided by Mercury, an imagination with the gifts of Venus, a heart that can warm like the Sun.

Since taking this ecstatic journey with Cosmiel, I no longer fear death. Instead I know of the wonders that lie in store for me, once freed of the physical body. Death, I now know, is a process of shedding, of letting go of attachments, of longings, of defences, of garments of thought and feeling that cover the pure radiance of the soul.

When it is time for me to be born again, I will take on the coverings I need to enable me to function in this world. Until that moment comes, to plunge once more into the realm of the Earth, with her joys and her sorrows, my soul will live in freedom in a world of bliss and joy.

IMAGES BY ANGELA LEMAIRE

p. 8   Etching aquatint *Reliance on the Angel*

p. 10   Wood-engraving *The Cat Who Went to Heaven*

p. 12   Wood-engraving *The Traveller*

p. 13   Pen and wash drawing *Angels Help Mankind*

p. 16   Linocut *Star Man*

p. 19   Wood-engraving *Dancing the Hills*

p. 21   Wood-engraving *Mandala*

p. 27   Engraving *Melancholia*

p. 33   Wood engraving *I found myself in a garden of graces*

p. 37   Engraving *The World Tree*

p. 39   Wood-engraving *Swan and Fan*

Angela Lemaire is a printmaker and painter
www.angelalemaire.co.uk

This work is an excerpt from *The Prophecies - A Novel* by Philip Carr-Gomm.

'An extraordinary work of the compassionate imagination.'
Lindsay Clarke, author The Chymical Wedding

'A powerful romance, on many levels - part political thriller, part esoteric journey, and part moving love story. I couldn't put it down.'
William Ayot, author Re-enchanting the Forest

'Masterfully combines elements of the transcendent with historical fact ... A hauntingly beautiful story...'
Rated Five Stars *****
San Francisco Book Review

'A brave book. Iconaclastic, disturbing and vivid. An eloquent journey beyond the boundaries that hold us all.'
Peter Owen-Jones, priest and author

'Mysterious. Magical. Erotic. An incredible story.'
Mark Townsend, author The Gospel of Falling Down

'Fascinating and completely engrossing.'
Barbara Erskine, Sunday Times Bestselling author

Available from Amazon

www.philipcarr-gomm.com

www.ingramcontent.com/pod-product-compliance
Lightning Source LLC
Chambersburg PA
CBHW031507040426
42444CB00007B/1245